D0772783

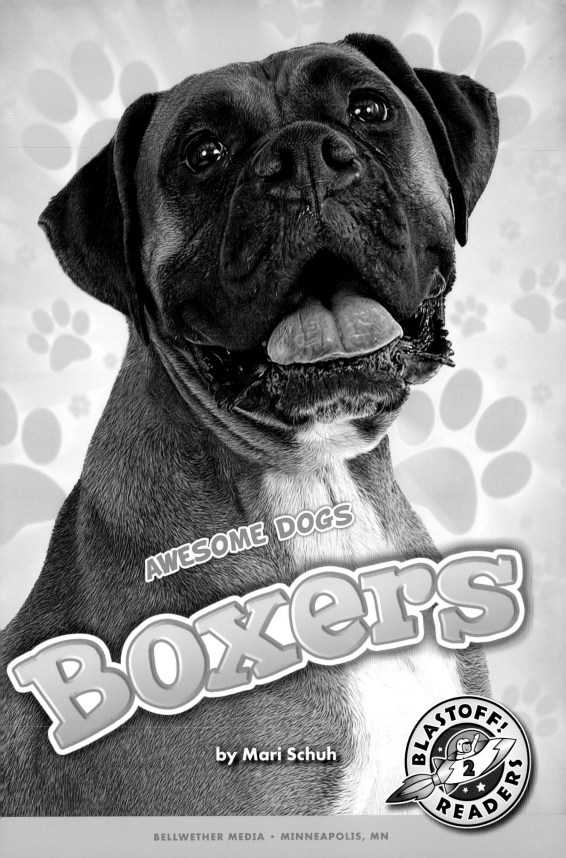

AWESOME DOGS

Boxers

by Mari Schuh

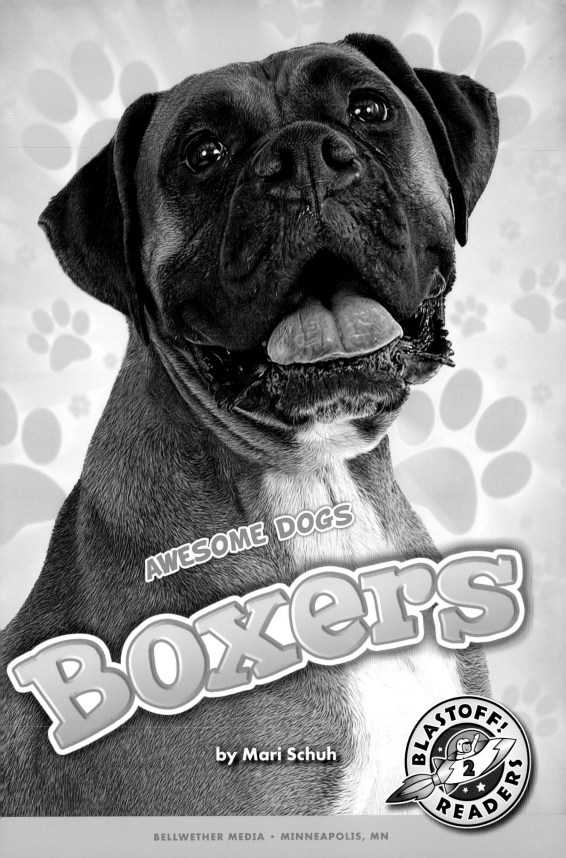
BLASTOFF!
2
READERS

BELLWETHER MEDIA • MINNEAPOLIS, MN

Note to Librarians, Teachers, and Parents:

Blastoff! Readers are carefully developed by literacy experts and combine standards-based content with developmentally appropriate text.

Level 1 provides the most support through repetition of high-frequency words, light text, predictable sentence patterns, and strong visual support.

Level 2 offers early readers a bit more challenge through varied simple sentences, increased text load, and less repetition of high-frequency words.

Level 3 advances early-fluent readers toward fluency through increased text and concept load, less reliance on visuals, longer sentences, and more literary language.

Level 4 builds reading stamina by providing more text per page, increased use of punctuation, greater variation in sentence patterns, and increasingly challenging vocabulary.

Level 5 encourages children to move from "learning to read" to "reading to learn" by providing even more text, varied writing styles, and less familiar topics.

Whichever book is right for your reader, Blastoff! Readers are the perfect books to build confidence and encourage a love of reading that will last a lifetime!

This edition first published in 2016 by Bellwether Media, Inc.

No part of this publication may be reproduced in whole or in part without written permission of the publisher. For information regarding permission, write to Bellwether Media, Inc., Attention: Permissions Department, 5357 Penn Avenue South, Minneapolis, MN 55419.

Library of Congress Cataloging-in-Publication Data
Schuh, Mari C., 1975- author.
  Boxers / by Mari Schuh.
    pages cm. – (Blastoff! Readers. Awesome Dogs)
  Summary: "Relevant images match informative text in this introduction to boxers. Intended for students in kindergarten through third grade"–Provided by publisher.
  Audience: Ages 5-8.
  Audience: K to grade 3.
  Includes bibliographical references and index.
  ISBN 978-1-62617-303-3 (hardcover : alk. paper)
  1. Boxer (Dog breed)–Juvenile literature. 2. Dog breeds–Juvenile literature. I. Title. II. Series: Blastoff! Readers. 2, Awesome Dogs.
  SF429.B75S38 2016
  636.73–dc23
                                    2015031584

Printed in the United States of America, North Mankato, MN.

Table of Contents

What Are Boxers?

Boxers are a strong, muscular dog **breed**.

4

They are **alert** and full of energy.

Boxers are medium-sized dogs.
They weigh between 55 and 70
pounds (25 and 32 kilograms).

They have long legs
and strong chests.
Their tails can be
long or short.

Boxers have **wrinkles** on their foreheads and **muzzles**. Their muzzles are short and square.

muzzle

Some boxers have floppy ears.
Others have ears that stand up.

Boxers have short, smooth **coats**.

Boxer Coats

fawn

brindle

Most are **fawn** or **brindle** in color. Some have white markings.

History of Boxers

In the 1800s, people in Germany first **bred** boxers. They mixed bulldogs, mastiffs, and other breeds.

Germany

Boxers worked with the police and military in Germany. They were one of the first breeds to do so!

Boxers may have been named for how they use their paws.

They stand up on their back legs.
Then they **box** with their front
paws when they play.

Today, some boxers are guard dogs and **service dogs**.

Boxer Profile

short coat

square muzzle

long legs

Life Span: 10 to 12 years

Trainability:

1 2 3 4 5 6

Hardest to train   Easiest to train

The **American Kennel Club** puts the breed in its **Working Group**.

Boxers are smart, active pets. They need a lot of exercise.

Boxers like to play fetch and go for long walks.

Boxers are fun and playful. They enjoy being around people.

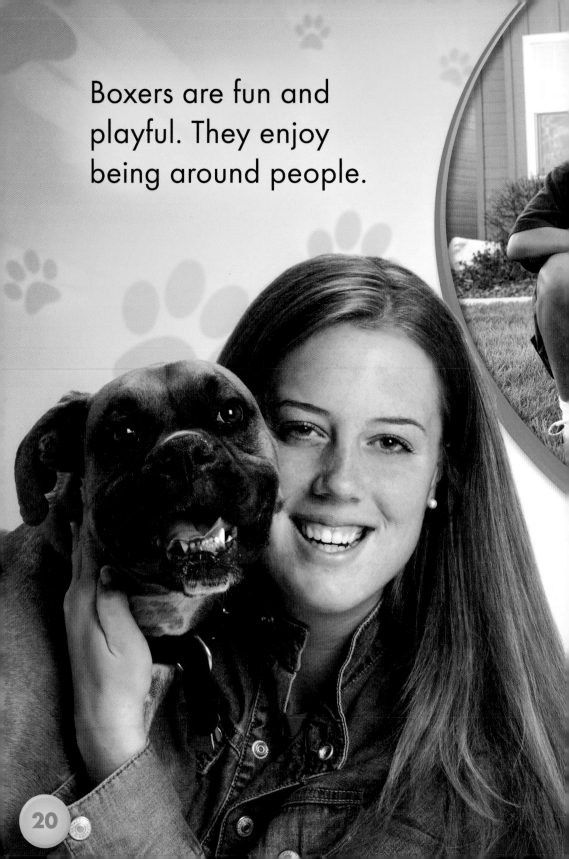

These dogs are calm and gentle with children. Boxers are **loyal** family pets!

Glossary

alert—quick to notice or act

American Kennel Club—an organization that keeps track of dog breeds in the United States

box—to hit or punch

bred—purposely mated two dogs to make puppies with certain qualities

breed—a type of dog

brindle—a solid coat color mixed with streaks or spots of another color

coats—the hair or fur covering some animals

fawn—a light brown color

loyal—having constant support for someone

muzzles—the noses and mouths of animals

service dogs—dogs trained to help people who have special needs perform daily tasks

Working Group—a group of dog breeds that have a history of performing jobs for people

wrinkles—lines in skin or fur

To Learn More

AT THE LIBRARY

Landau, Elaine. *Boxers Are the Best!* Minneapolis, Minn.: Lerner Publications Co., 2010.

Rustad, Martha E. H. *Dogs*. North Mankato, Minn.: Capstone Press, 2015.

Shores, Erika L. *All About Boxers*. North Mankato, Minn.: Capstone Press, 2013.

ON THE WEB

Learning more about boxers is as easy as 1, 2, 3.

1. Go to www.factsurfer.com.

2. Enter "boxers" into the search box.

3. Click the "Surf" button and you will see a list of related web sites.

With factsurfer.com, finding more information is just a click away.

Index

The images in this book are reproduced through the courtesy of: Susan Schmitz, front cover; Dora Zett, p. 4; Bigandt, p. 5; Lenkadan, p. 6; Ron Kimball/ Kimball Stock, p. 7; cynoclub, p. 8; Lynn M. Stone/ Kimball Stock, p. 9; vdovin_vn, p. 10; MarkCoffeyPhoto, p. 11 (left); Suzi Nelson, p. 11 (right); Dora Zett, p. 12; Tierfotoagentur/ Alamy, pp. 13, 18; Anna Hoychuk, p. 14; Cristina Bellitti/ Kimball Stock, p. 15; Whytock, p. 16; Gelpi JM, p. 17; otsphoto, p. 19; Rob Bartee/ Alamy, p. 20; Hurst Photo, p. 21.